More Praise for *Intuition for Starters*

Having just experienced a situation in which I thought my intuition had utterly failed me, I'm indebted to this book for clarifying what intuition actually is and for giving solid guidance in becoming more intuitive. This book is an excellent beginning point for anyone who wants to understand or better utilize innate yet undeveloped intuitive skills.

—-D. Kate Jewell, NAPRA ReView

Intuition is our birthright. This clear and powerful book teaches us how to tap into the incredible wisdom it offers and integrate that wisdom into our daily life. Get ready: your entire life view and experiences are about to change dramatically.

—-Carol Ritberger, Ph.D. author of
What Color is Your Personality

Finally, an intuition book that actually works! This is, by far, the clearest, most concise introduction to this important topic that I've read. These techniques will change your life.

—Jyotish Novak, author of *How to Meditate*

INTUITION
for STARTERS

❖

How to Know and Trust
Your Inner Guidance

J. Donald Walters

EDITED BY

DEVI NOVAK

Crystal Clarity Publishers
Nevada City, CA

ISBN: 1-56589-155-4
Cover and book design by C.A. Starner Schuppe
1 3 5 7 9 10 8 6 4 2

Printed in Canada

CRYSTAL

CLARITY

Crystal Clarity Publishers
14618 Tyler Foote Rd.
Nevada City, CA 95959

800-424-1055
www.crystalclarity.com
clarity@crystalclarity.com

Library of Congress Cataloging-in-Publication Data

Walters, J. Donald.
  Intuition for starters : how to know and trust your inner guidance /
J. Donald Walters ; edited by Devi Novak.
      p. cm.
Includes bibliographical references.
  ISBN 1-56589-155-4
  1. Intuition. I. Novak, Devi. II. Title.
  BF315.5 .W35 2002
  153.4'4--dc21

                                                    2002003518

Contents

❖

Introduction

❖

This little book can change your life—it's certainly changed mine as the editor. It offers solutions to many of our most basic questions: How do I know what are the right decisions? How can I better understand other people? What is the purpose of my life? How do I fit into the larger scheme of things?

These questions often challenge and baffle us all. Without some source of inner guidance, making decisions can seem like trying to untie a jumbled knot of thread— the more we pull the ends, the tighter the knot becomes. Using the techniques presented here, you'll be able to unravel the sometimes-confusing tangle of problems you're faced with, and act with assurance that you're drawing on true guidance.

The exciting thing about working with these techniques is that they can transform the way we think and respond to just about everything we do. Creative solutions can be found for every situation in our life, and new answers to old questions appear.

Working with intuition not only enables us to live more successfully, but it can become a *way* of life—filled with greater enthusiasm and energy to face the challenges that may confront us. As one highly successful person said, "There are no obstacles in life, only opportunities." This can be our motto, too, once we're able to step out of the shadows of doubt and uncertainty, and face every new situation with the confidence born of inner clarity.

But there's also a deeper benefit that you'll receive by reading this book and practicing its principles—you can begin to explore your own higher levels of consciousness. True guidance comes from an expanded state of awareness that is always operating just beneath our conscious mind, called the superconscious. From this state we can tap into a powerful stream of energy and creative solutions in our life. We're able to grasp subtle truths in the world around us, and can feel a greater unity with life. Tuning in to superconsciousness does more than help us know what decisions to make: it helps us know who we really are.

J. Donald Walters, the author of this book, has spent more than fifty years living these truths and sharing them with students throughout the world. Personally trained by the great master of yoga, Paramhansa Yogananda, Mr. Walters draws his teachings from a tradition that has enabled people down through the millennia to experience their own highest potential.

What's so convincing about the value of these techniques is the example of Mr. Walters' own life. Practicing principles for drawing intuitive guidance for many years, Mr. Walters has been able to accomplish extraordinary things: writing over eighty books and 400 pieces of music, founding a number of successful intentional communities, and offering wise counsel and guidance to thousands of students and friends worldwide.

Within each of us lies the ability to attract the answers we need for the challenges that confront us. *Intuition for Starters* will set your feet on a new road of knowing how to draw creative solutions, and of realizing that life is not an endless array of problems. It's a great adventure filled with unimagined possibilities and untarnished hope.

Devi Novak
Ananda World Brotherhood Village
Nevada City, California

INTUITION
for STARTERS

CHAPTER ONE

❖

What Is Intuition, and Where Does It Come From?

When we look at the world around us, we find a celebration of life in the universe—shining through the stars, singing through the birds, laughing through children, and dancing with the wind in the trees. With all this beauty and diversity surrounding us, we sometimes yearn to feel more a part of it all. We want to sing in harmony with the "music of the spheres." What happens all too often, alas, is merely that we add discord by adhering adamantly to our own ego-generated notes.

We've all seen groups of little children singing. There's usually one child who has no idea of the melody being sung, but he or she wants so desperately to be a part of the activity, that he sings enthusiastically whatever notes he likes, adding charm, if not harmony, to the music. Perhaps less innocently than that child, we intrude our private wishes saying, "I want the world to be *this* way," or, "Come on, everybody, let's do it *my* way." In consequence, the world is full of disharmony, and we hear the cacophony on all sides.

How may we tune into the greater symphony of life? A friend of mine, when confronted with any new situation, approaches the problem this way: He asks, "What is trying to happen here?" How often do we insist, instead, on changing reality to meet our own desires? In the process, we lose sight of the over-all purpose. We struggle to make sense of life segment by segment instead of as an over-all flow. Viewing everything fragmentarily, like pieces of a jigsaw puzzle, no coherent picture emerges, no path, and no direction to guide our understanding.

There is a way for us to find that path, however—to feel a part of that greater reality, and therefore to know what is right for us as individuals. That way involves opening ourselves and becoming receptive to higher potentials of consciousness within ourselves, and thereby of living in harmony with the world around us. It involves developing our own inner sense of intuitive guidance.

Intuition is the innate ability in everyone to perceive truth directly—not by reason, logic, or analysis, but by a simple knowing from within. That is the very meaning of the word "intuition": to know, or understand *from within*—from one's own self, and from the heart of whatever one is trying to understand. Intuition is the inner ability to see behind the outer forms of things to their inner essence.

We've all experienced occasional "lucky hunches," when we knew what street to take or what card to choose in a game without understanding how or why.

This intuitive ability is latent within all of us. It can be developed consciously to bring clarity to all our decisions.

Intuition is neither feminine nor masculine. Sometimes we hear people talk about "feminine intuition," because intuition relates more to the feeling aspect of human nature, but, in fact, it is equally present in both men and women. I've observed, interestingly, that women are often more intuitive in their understanding of other people, whereas men are more so in the area of their work. But the truth is that intuition is *calm*, impersonal feeling. Women often experience life more by feeling in the form of emotions; men often tend to be more impersonal. A combination of the two qualities is what produces intuition.

For better or worse, every decision we make is influenced. It isn't possible not to be guided at all for the simple reason that we ourselves are fragments of a greater reality. We can say, however, "I choose to be guided by that which leads to my own and others' true happiness, rather than by that which ends in cul-de-sacs of suffering."

How are we influenced in the decisions we make? In part, it's our exposure to the mass consciousness of others around us, which affects us on obvious as well as on subtle levels. I'm not referring merely to the subliminal messages one receives while thumbing through a magazine or watching television. The influences I refer to are subtler still, and more powerful. We can't avoid them by shutting out sensory stimuli, because the very thoughts people think are all pervasive and deeply affect our consciousness.

Years ago in San Francisco, I had a very quiet apartment. At twelve o'clock noon it was as quiet as at three in the morning. It was interesting to note, however, that at three in the morning, there was a greater, pervading silence. I don't mean silence only to the ears, but to the mind, because people everywhere were asleep. The thoughts of those around you, even more than their words and the obvious messages they put out, definitely affect the way we act and think.

We can't escape these influences. We can, however, determine *how* they affect us, responding to those that lead to beneficial results of success in life and inner fulfillment. Influences that might bring less fortunate consequences can be filtered out by intuitive insight and recognized for what they really are—seeming to proffer upliftment, while in the end, like opium, bringing devastation.

The Three Levels of Consciousness

We filter what influences us according to our habitual level of awareness. The totality of our consciousness is comprised of three levels: the subconscious, the conscious, and the superconscious. These levels of consciousness represent differing degrees of *intensity* of awareness. As we move from one level to another, different kinds of influences will most affect us.

The first level, the subconscious, is relatively dim in awareness: it is the stuff of which dreams are made. We may think of it as the repository of all remembered experiences, impressions left on the mind by those experiences, and tendencies awakened or reinforced by those impressions. Every experience we've ever had, every thought, every impression of loss or gain, resides in the subconscious mind and determines our patterns of thought and behavior far more than we realize.

The subconscious, being unrestricted by the rigid demands of logic, permits a certain flow of ideas. This flow may border on intuition, but if the ideas are too circumscribed by subjectivity, they won't correspond with the external world around us. When we dream at night, we are mainly operating on the subconscious level. I remember a dream I had once many years ago in which I was flying. I thought, "This isn't what people do! How can I be flying?" Then the thought came to me, "Maybe I'm dreaming!" So I decided to think it through carefully: Was I awake? Or was I asleep? Reasoning it through logically, I decided on what seemed to me a perfectly rational conclusion that I was awake: I was only doing something out of the ordinary. A moment later I woke up: What was my surprise to find that in actuality I'd been asleep all the time!

Animals operate primarily on the subconscious level. In their fluid awareness, they have a certain degree of intuition. People who ride horses often find them responding instantly to their thoughts. A horse will often know as soon as you get in the saddle, if you're a good rider or not; it immediately senses who's in control.

I heard a story (related as true) about a cat that lived with a family in Wisconsin. The family had to move to Washington State some 1500 miles away. Deciding they couldn't take the cat with them, they reluctantly left it with a neighbor. They settled down in their new home and were there several months when, one morning, the cat appeared on their doorstep. He'd been able by intuition to follow and find them. You certainly can't attribute that to a developed sense of smell—just imagine the cat sniffing its way along the highway! Something else was at work: the cat's intuition!

When we're talking about animals, and even unaware actions of human beings, it's a mistake to speak of the "unconscious," as psychologists have done. There is no such thing as "unconsciousness." A universal consciousness, or God, has produced everything in existence. Even the rocks have consciousness—granted a low degree of it, but the least germ of consciousness exists in every atom.

We can think of ourselves as atoms evolved finally to the level of *self-awareness*. At our stage of evolution, it's natural for the awakened consciousness in us to reach out with more dynamic awareness to even higher levels of consciousness. At first in this process, however, we may be only dimly aware that this is what we are doing.

The subconscious mind can all too easily intrude itself on our conscious awareness, tricking us into thinking we're getting intuitive guidance, when actually we're merely being influenced by past impressions and unfulfilled desires. The subconscious mind is in some ways close to the superconscious, where real intuition resides. Both represent a flow of awareness without logical obstructions. The subconscious is therefore more open to the intuitions of the superconscious, and sometimes receives them, though usually mixed with confusing imagery. To be really clear in the guidance we receive is difficult, but very important. Calamitous decisions have been made in the belief that one was drawing on higher guidance, when in fact one was responding only to subconscious preconditioning.

The next level of consciousness from which we receive guidance is the conscious state, the rational awareness that usually guides our daily decisions. When we receive input from the senses, analyze the facts, and make decisions based on this information, we are using this conscious level of guidance. This process is also strongly affected by the opinions of others, which can cloud our ability to draw true guidance.

Dividing and separating the world into either/or categories, the conscious level of awareness is problem-oriented. It's difficult to be completely certain of decisions drawn from this level, because the analytical mind can see all the possible solutions. But ultimately it doesn't have the ability to distinguish which one is best. If we rely exclusively on the conscious mind, we may find ourselves lacking in certainty and slipping into a state of perpetual indecision. We may find ourselves constantly wondering, "But what if this happens?" or "Perhaps that other way would have been better."

I've noticed a certain habitual response from people who primarily use the conscious mind in decision-making when they come to me for advice. If I offer a possible solution, their usual reply is, "Yes, but . . . Well, maybe on the other hand. . . ." If I suggest the answer they're seeking may lie in one direction, they'll counter with the possibility of other alternatives. They go around in circles and never seem to find a clear course of action.

Between the conscious and subconscious minds, dividing but also uniting them, lies a third level of awareness: the superconscious. This state begins at the fine dividing line between sleep and wakefulness. If you can catch your mind just at the moment when you are falling asleep, or at that fleeting instant before your consciousness rises to full wakefulness, you may find that you can slip gently into semi-superconsciousness, or enter into full superconsciousness.

Intuition and heightened mental clarity flow from superconscious awareness. The conscious mind is limited by its analytical nature, and therefore sees all things as separate and distinct. We may be puzzled by a certain situation, but because it seems unrelated to other events, it's difficult to draw a clear course of action. By contrast, because the superconscious mind is unitive and sees all things as part of a whole, it can readily draw solutions. In superconsciousness the problem and the solution are seen as one, as though the solution was a natural outgrowth from the problem.

Though the state of superconsciousness is latent in every individual, it's still unrealized in most people. By contacting it, we can become aware of our interconnection with everyone and with all life. Paramhansa Yogananda, a master in the science of yoga and meditation, could enter the superconscious state at will. He wrote a beautiful poem in which he describes this state of oneness with all as knowing the "thoughts of all men, past, present, to come."

In his *Autobiography of a Yogi*, Yogananda also described this state as "Center everywhere, circumference nowhere." When we reach our own inner center, we realize that the center of all beings is a part of our consciousness, and that nothing exists outside of that. Our intuition can effortlessly perceive the essence of any problem and the appropriate solution when we tap in to the superconscious state. Far from cutting us off from needs of others, superconscious awareness reflects the realities of all. Everything we do, then, is in harmony with the symphony of life, and in some way results in benefit for all.

Modern Western history largely reflects the predominance of logical, scientific over intuitive, superconscious perception. Today scientists presume to understand the universe by logic alone, because they assume that its laws are discernible exclusively by logic. But can logic alone create a poem or a symphony, or even bring a scientist a new discovery? The answer to this question is "no."

Albert Einstein, perhaps the greatest scientific mind of our time, said that any true scientist needs a sense of mystical wonder and awe before the universe if he hopes to understand it. While yet a young man, he made his discovery of the Theory of Relativity based on an insight that came to him in an intuitive flash. He then struggled for many years to explain it logically to others, so that they too could understand it.

Similarly when we read about the great discoveries of science throughout history, they've all been based primarily on intuition. Perhaps the scientists followed a logical process from A to B to C, but then suddenly there was an inexplicable leap from C to Q. They try to explain the discovery rationally because they believe in the logical process, but ultimately it's intuition from the superconscious level that made the breakthrough.

An Exercise to Tap
into the Superconscious Mind

Superconsciousness has its bodily center in the frontal lobe of the brain. The conscious state operates from the middle part of the brain; and the subconscious, from the lower brain. Thus, there is a kind of linear progression of awareness from subconsciousness toward superconsciousness. We can develop the ability to pass at will from one state of consciousness to another. A helpful practice in this regard is to ally your state of consciousness with the position of your eyes.

You will find, when you look down, that the mind tends more easily to drift into subconsciousness. When you look straight ahead, it is easier to shake off sleep's lethargy. And when you look up, it is easier to soar into higher consciousness and to feel higher guidance.

Practice this exercise:

1) Look down, closing your eyes. Feel yourself drifting downward as if sinking through water—through forests of waving seaweed—ever deeper

into a green, misty world of fantasy. Enjoy this pleasant sense of freedom from earthly responsibility, from demanding projects, from fears, from worldly ambitions. Affirm mentally, "Through slowly drifting waters, I sink into subconsciousness."

2) Now, with a quick burst of will power, open your eyes and gaze straight ahead. Shake off the last clinging tendrils of passivity. Affirm, "With a burst of energy I rise to greet the world!"

3) Remain in that state a few moments. Then look upward and affirm, "I awake in Thy light! I am joyful! I am free! I awake in Thy light!"

Practice alternating between these three states of consciousness, accompanying them with a corresponding shift in the position of your eyes. Gradually, you will gain the ability to control your states of consciousness at will, and choose the level of guidance you receive.

❖

How to Tune in to Intuitive Guidance

The superconscious, conscious, and subconscious minds all operate from different parts of the brain. By practicing the exercise we've learned in the last chapter, we can become more aware of which part we're using while doing different activities. Try noticing where in the brain your consciousness is centered while relaxing or drifting off to sleep, while driving in busy traffic, or when feeling particularly joyful or uplifted.

Awareness of different areas of the brain is only a part of tuning in to the superconscious mind. The science of yoga teaches that we actually have *three* bodies: the physical body; the astral, or "energy" body, seat of our mental and emotional natures; and the idea or "causal" body, which operates in the realm of pure thought.

We are, of course, readily aware of our physical bodies, but we can also find evidence of the existence of the astral body when looking at Kirlian photographs. In photos of people's hands, for example, one can see a beautifully colored image of energy radiating out from the physical form. In differing photos, the radiant image is larger or smaller, brighter or dimmer depending on the strength and quality of the person's energy.

The astral body has seven "energy centers," or *chakras* as they are called in Sanskrit, that govern various aspects of our mental and emotional states. These vortices of energy are located along our "astral" spine, which is the energy counterpart to our physical spine and brain. If you're interested in learning more about the chakras, I recommend you read *Chakras for Starters,* available from Crystal Clarity Publishers.

Two of these chakras are particularly important in tuning in to intuitive guidance: the *anahata* chakra, or dorsal center, located in the area of the physical heart, and the *ajna* chakra, or Spiritual Eye, located at the point between the eyebrows. When in meditation, as we concentrate at the Spiritual Eye, we're focusing our consciousness on the frontal lobes of the brain where the superconscious mind is located.

Exercises for Greater Awareness of the Chakras

Here are some exercises to help you become more aware of the *anahata* and *ajna* chakras. In preparation, begin by sitting up with a straight spine, and trying to still the restless thoughts in the mind. Now practice a yoga technique called Regular Breathing: Inhale to a count of 12, hold the breath for 12 counts, and exhale to a count of twelve. Do this for six to twelve rounds. Then throw the breath out, and sit quietly for a few moments.

Now focus your attention on the *anahata* chakra, located in the area behind the physical heart. Draw your shoulder blades together several times by tensing and relaxing the area of the back behind the heart. Visualize a great sphere of light expanding outward from the area of your heart. Feel this sphere encompassing everything around you—your house, neighborhood, country, the world, and all of space. Try to feel that everyone and everything is bathed in this light. Sit quietly and keeping your body relaxed, try to feel an actual sensation of warmth or energy in the *anahata* chakra.

*   *   *   *   *

Now bring your attention to the *ajna* chakra, or the point between the eyebrows. Knit your brows together several times to stimulate the energy here. Concentrate on projecting a beam of light from this point, like the light coming from the projection booth in a movie theatre. Feel this beam moving outward through space with great power, driving away all shadows of pain and sorrow. Use your will power to send this light further and further into space. Now relax and feel a radiant center of light and energy at the point between the eyebrows.

*　　　*　　　*　　　*　　　*

These two chakras act as sending and receiving stations for our thoughts and feelings, just like a radio transmitter and receiver. In his book, *Autobiography of a Yogi*, Paramhansa Yogananda says, "The human mind, free from the static of restlessness, can perform through its antenna of intuition all the functions of complicated radio mechanisms—sending and receiving thoughts, and tuning out undesirable ones. As the power of a radio depends on the amount of electrical current it can utilize, so the human radio is energized according to the power of will possessed by each individual."

Technique for Tuning in to Intuitive Guidance

Here is a very effective technique for tuning in to guidance using these two chakras:

1) Concentrate at the *ajna* chakra, the point between the eyebrows, which is the sending station for our thoughts. Now ask for guidance from the superconsciousness. You can send out a strong thought like, "What shall I do?"

2) Wait for a response in the receiving station of intuition, the *anahata* or heart center. Be completely impartial, and try to feel a yes or no answer. It will become increasingly clear as you work on developing it. Sometimes that feeling will be very definite, but if it isn't clear there are things you can do to clarify the response you've received. Try posing alternate solutions, and see if one feels right in your heart. Remember, the answer doesn't come on a mental level. You can't think yourself to it. You have to suspend thought,

and get it on an intuitive level. I've often found that the answer will come clearly at the very end of my period of asking for guidance. Sometimes I'll receive it days later when walking or relaxing, and not really expecting it.

3) Finally, a problem is half-solved already once it is stated clearly. In seeking guidance, form a clear mental picture of the question you have. Then hold that picture up to the superconsciousness at the point between the eyebrows. People often struggle for a long time to find the guidance they want. No time is really needed: only sufficient mental clarity and energy.

The Art of It

This is the basic technique, but there are subtle refinements that you need in order to practice it effectively. First, let's talk about the importance of high energy. Just as the flow of electricity in a wire creates a magnetic field, so too our thoughts produce a flow of energy that creates a magnetic field. The strength and quality of this energy determines the clarity as well as the kinds of answers we receive. If I want to write a piece of music, for example, I try to tune in to a musical feeling, and then with great energy ask the superconscious for a melody. In this way I've been able to compose hundreds of pieces of music quite quickly and easily.

Remember the superconscious mind is solution-oriented. You, too, must be solution-oriented to draw guidance, and you must have the courage to ask. Try to free your mind from the static of doubt, and strongly hold the thought, "There is an answer, and it *will* come to me if I seek in the right way." This is what Jesus meant when he said, "Pray believing." When we energetically offer our thoughts to the superconscious level with confidence that the answer will be there, true guidance readily comes.

Another important point is to always pose questions to the superconscious in a positive way. Don't say as though anticipating a failure, "Why don't I get an answer?" This negative kind of approach actually tends to paralyze the flow of intuition. Rather say with expectancy, "The answer is . . . ," and you'll find that the solution will be there. When there is confidence, patience, and positive determination the right answer will come in time.

Even with the best efforts, however, we don't always get a clear answer. What can we do then? Start by becoming inwardly calm, and trying to get yourself out of the way. Strongly hold the thought that you don't have any preferences about which answer you're going to receive. If you want to get true guidance, it's important that there be no attachment to a particular response or any desire to influence the outcome.

Then pose various options, and see which feels right. Try to visualize the alternatives as distinctly as possible, because if your thoughts aren't clear, then you won't get a clear answer either. Put a great deal of will power into visualizing the different options, and one will emerge with strong positive energy around it.

In this process it's important to be as impartial as possible. When you hold up alternatives to the super-conscious mind, don't put your bet secretly on one choice over another. When the answer comes, even if it's not the "horse" you bet on, have the courage to follow it. After receiving inner guidance, many people will reject the outcome, saying, "I didn't want *that* one." Over time this attitude will constrict the flow of guidance you receive.

There was a cartoon of somebody calling up to heaven, "Is anybody up there?" A voice thundered down from the clouds, "Yes, my child, I am here." Then the person asked, "What should I do with my life?" The answer came, "I want you to live an honest and chaste life." The person paused, and then asked, "Is anybody *else* up there?"

So after offering up various alternatives, consult your heart to feel which one of them seems best. Go with that, but keep checking to make sure your guidance continues to feel right. In the beginning you may often make mistakes in recognizing true guidance, but keep trying and listening, and gradually you'll come to know what your intuition is telling you.

Unfortunately, people sometimes adopt an attitude of

presumption or inflexibility about what they feel is higher guidance. Before we can hope to be rightly guided, it's important to be humble and open to the possibility of being wrong. When you can accept other ways of doing things, you're much more likely to be guided correctly than if you're convinced that your way absolutely has to be right. There's always the possibility that the solution is far greater in scope than what may have occurred to you.

There's a story of a man who died and went to heaven. St. Peter was showing the newcomer around, and took him to what was called the "heavenly junkyard." This was the place where all the things that had been rejected by people on earth were collected. After seeing some wonderful things there, the man said in amazement, "This isn't possible! Look at that Rolls Royce over there! Who would reject such a thing?"

St Peter said, "It's interesting that you should ask about that, because the person who rejected it once was *you*!" The man was shocked. "That's impossible! What do you mean?" St. Peter replied, "Well, whenever you asked for a car, you always visualized a Volkswagen." Superconscious guidance may exceed the logical conclusions of the conscious mind.

If you've been trying to draw guidance, but can't get clarity on a point because you're upset or have become too close to the problem, that's the time to say to yourself, "I'm not getting the answer by worrying about it, so let me do other things for now. When I'm calm and a bit more detached, I'll take this problem off the shelf and deal with it." True intuition can never come when we're in a state of emotional turmoil.

When you're having trouble getting guidance, it's important to realize that sometimes it isn't the right time to receive an answer. Other events may have to be resolved before clarity will come in that area. When this occurs it's helpful to keep bringing the question to the superconscious mind, but without any expectations. Have confidence that the answer will come to you at the right time.

Someone wisely said, "Asking for guidance is like planting a seed in the ground. If you keep digging it up every day to see if it's sprouted, it will never germinate." So plant the seeds of your requests in the soil of your superconsciousness, and let them come to fruition in their own time.

Another important point is being open to what others have to say. Ask your friends for guidance, especially those you trust who've proved their sense of good judgment over time. I had a friend who was a great help to me when I wrote music. She had a very good knack for sensing when something wasn't quite right. I'd telephone her with a new song I was working on, and she'd say something like, "It's very nice, but can't you make that rhyme a little cleaner?" Then I'd work at it, and suddenly find that it was much better.

In your openness to input from others, however, don't lose your own center or the sense of what's right for you. If you repeatedly say to everyone, "What do you think? Gee, I don't know what to do," you may end up doing nothing. As somebody said once, "Don't be so open-minded that your brains spill out." If we behave like weather vanes, going with any breeze that comes along, we'll never find true guidance.

Remember that working with intuition isn't just a Monday afternoon kind of thing—it's all-week round and all-year round. If we ask for guidance only when we're in a crisis, the chances are slim that we'll be able to draw clear answers. It could happen, but most often it's the people who are always open to higher guidance that readily receive it.

Try consciously to work with your intuition all the time, and you'll find that it can help you in every aspect of your life. At work, for example, if you're trying to make a decision about whether to hire somebody for a job, try visualizing their eyes at the point between your eyebrows. Then feel in your heart what qualities they project from their eyes. If you're sufficiently calm and focused, you'll feel in your heart a positive, negative, or even a neutral reaction. Some people may seem very nice at first, but if you look sensitively into their eyes, you may see there's something wrong with their consciousness.

Tapping into superconsciousness is like logging our computer on to the mainframe of a vast database: it gives us access to unlimited possibilities and solutions. But tuning in to intuitive guidance isn't just a mechanical act like searching for information on the Internet. The superconscious mind is conscious and self-aware. The more we try to attune to it, the more it will respond to our needs and provide us with the answers we're seeking.

CHAPTER THREE

❖

How to Trust Your Intuition

How can we learn to recognize when we've received true guidance? This point is almost impossible to convey with absolute certainty, because it's a subjective experience. When teaching art, for example, you can share everything about painting except how to be a great artist—that's something you can't put into words. There are many art students who take the same classes from the same professors, but only one may emerge as a great artist while the others remain mediocre. The inner essence of any activity can't be taught directly, but needs to be intuited by the student from within.

I experienced this many years ago when I began taking singing lessons. My teacher said, "The voice is the one instrument you can't see, so I can't *show* you how to sing. But if you sing correctly, and try to attune yourself to the way I'm placing my voice, gradually you'll be able to do it right." She would sing a note, and then have me repeat it. Then she'd sing it again, and I'd repeat it again. This went on for many months, and although I showed improvement, she still wasn't completely satisfied.

Finally at the end of six months, she stopped me in the middle of a song and cried out with great satisfaction, "That note! That's the way all your notes should sound!" At that moment I inwardly *felt* what she had been trying to convey about voice placement. It was a great gift to be trained by such a teacher, because she gave me a true understanding of how to use my voice.

The ability to know inwardly what will work in any undertaking comes partly with experience. Somebody who's been doing an activity for a long time will automatically know what choice to make, because experience hones the sharp edge of intuition. A businessman who's worked for years in his field will know instantly what course to take, because experience has given him an intuitive sense about it. He'll recognize what is really right as opposed to what only seems right. Though that sense is difficult to convey to anyone else, as you exercise your intuition over time, you'll gradually become aware of the kind of feeling that indicates the right choice.

This feeling is very subtle, and one that will be perceived differently by each of us. Even after years of trying to tune in to higher guidance, I still approach it cautiously. When people first begin working with their intuition, I find that they can become too affirmative about it. You'll find them saying things like, "I *know* this must be so. My inner guidance told me." I tend to be a little skeptical when people say things like that, because when you really feel something with certainty, you don't need to proclaim it to the world. It's best to sensitively hold on to that feeling, and continue to listen quietly within yourself for further intuitive guidance.

What To Look For

First of all, to recognize the kind of feeling that indicates true guidance, look for three qualities: calmness, clarity, and joy. Intuition is always based in a deep sense of calmness and detachment. When you're trying to tune in to the superconscious mind, ask yourself if the guidance you've received makes you feel excited or restless. If so, then it's safe to assume that you're just going along with your own desires. Try to associate true guidance with a sense of calm acceptance. When you've received an answer rather than thinking, "Yes, YES, YESS!", your attitude should be, "Whatever is, is. It doesn't touch me personally."

You'll experience a certain power with inner calmness, but it's also very steady. If you find yourself jumping up and down in an agitated state, thinking, "Oh boy!

I got this guidance. It's just great!!" then it's probably worth questioning.

The second thing to associate with true intuition is a sense of clarity. If you're visualizing different alternatives, or if guidance comes to you in a dream, it's important to distinguish between subconscious and superconscious influences. Subconscious images tend to have a certain obscurity or cloudiness to them, and the colors appear dim or muddy. These signs indicate projections of the subconscious mind and shouldn't be trusted. In super-conscious experiences, the colors will be bright, pure, and brilliant, and the images filled with clarity or radiance. The clarity of colors and images are strong signs that you've tuned in to true intuition.

Finally, look for a sense of inner joy. The basis of this kind of joy should be calmness and deep impartiality. If it makes you feel emotionally excited, then it probably only reflects the temporary happiness that comes when our desires are fulfilled. True guidance should have a joy that takes you inside rather than outside of yourself. Like a current of energy, this kind of joy should take your consciousness inward and upward—not inward in the sense of self-congratulation, but upward with a sense of soaring freedom.

In developing your ability to recognize intuition, it's important to test your guidance over a period of time. Unless you have no choice, don't make big decisions on the strength of intuition. It's better to begin with small decisions, and continually test your ability. You'll begin noticing that when a certain feeling comes, and you follow it, things work out well. Then there's a different feeling, less calm or clear. At first you may think it's got to be right, but over time you'll come to recognize this feeling as false guidance. Gradually you'll come to understand the difference from your own experience. You may not be able to explain to others how you know, but when you learn to recognize true guidance, it cannot fail you.

Another way to recognize intuition is to act it out and watch your reactions as you go. If you're doing the right thing, your inner feeling will gradually come stronger and clearer as you act. If you have no guidance at all, sometimes it is better just to start anyway, because often any action is better than none at all. But don't presume—take small steps. You'll find by doing a little, the energy starts to flow. As this happens, the guidance gradually comes into focus.

There's another method that has also worked for me over the years. If you're unsure of your guidance, try inwardly saying no to it and pushing it away. If the intuition continues to come back to you with strong energy, then it's probably more than just your own thoughts at work.

Don't Expect Absolutes

True guidance comes according to who you are and what you've asked, and rarely expresses itself in absolute terms. It's unlikely that a mathematician will receive guidance about the right color balance for a painting. Rather he'll receive it about mathematics—and if he speaks English, it will be in English.

Intuition reflects our own personal perspective. When we start out on a certain line of action, our guidance will come in response to that. When I'm trying to write music, my intuition guides me in that way, not about how to put in a new driveway. If it does come in that, I'll brush it aside because it's not what I'm looking for.

Different people can sometimes be guided in contrasting or even conflicting ways, because their interests and needs may vary. There's a strange story from the life of Paramhansa Yogananda when he was a young man in India. Because he was a very dynamic and magnetic person, many people looked to him for leadership. Once a group of young Indian men asked him to lead them in an uprising against the British. He replied, "No, God will free India in my lifetime by peaceful means." Through the practice of meditation, he intuitively knew that this statement was true. When one of the members of the group asked him to reconsider, Yogananda replied, "No, it's not right for me to do. But it's your karma—you do it." So this man decided to lead the group in their plans to overthrow the British.

A large consignment of arms was coming from

Germany into the harbor outside of Calcutta in the Bay of Bengal. With these guns they planned to arm enough people to stage an uprising. But the group was betrayed, and the British were alerted to the plot. When the boat docked the shipment of arms was seized, and all the people involved were caught and executed.

Years later when Yogananda told a group of us this story, I asked him, "Why did you tell him to do it, if you could see what the results would be?" "It was his karma," he replied. Yogananda, who had tremendous compassion for the sufferings of others, wasn't indifferent to what had befallen the man. But he was trying to teach us that each person has certain lessons to learn, and these differ according to our individual karma.

It was the right guidance for the young revolutionary because he was fulfilling his destiny. But for Yogananda, it was the wrong action—not because his life was spared, but because his destiny lay elsewhere. It was the right thing for that group, but the wrong thing for bringing political freedom to India.

Don't assume that if you're guided to do something,

that it's necessarily right for everybody. Be open to the fact that a different course may be needed for someone else. When people offer me what seems like good advice, I can sometimes see that though it would work well for them, it would be a disaster for me. In that case I'll reply, "This guidance may be true for you, but there are certain things I have to learn by taking another direction."

Negative Signs to Watch Out For

When asking for guidance, try to be aware of a feeling of blocked energy, or of a psychic threshold you can't cross over. Be sensitive to this, and don't try to blast your way through it. The voice of intuition is usually very quiet and calm, so it's often easy to ignore or shout down. Listen for the merest whisper and be prepared to follow it, because often it's the quietest voice of all that's most likely to be right.

If you feel a sense of nervousness or agitation about a course of action, it's best not to proceed. This doesn't necessarily mean that you should abandon the whole project, but perhaps only that a refinement is needed. I remember an experience I had once when writing a letter to someone who had asked for my advice. I was trying to draw my response from a sense of intuitive guidance, so that I could tune in to what this person really needed to hear. At one point I introduced a new element into the letter, and as soon as I did this, I felt a sense of nervousness in my heart. I thought, "Logically it seems right to put it in, but it doesn't feel right." As soon as I removed it, I felt calm again and finished the letter.

Another sign to watch for is the effects of your guidance on other people. If it feels right to you, but it's creating disharmony all around, then the direction is probably wrong. To understand this better, it may help you to make this distinction: Is it *the guidance* that's creating the problem because it's wrong in itself, or is the disharmony coming from others' misunderstanding?

If Jesus had looked at his life and assumed the first case, he might have said, "Gee, I made a mistake in trying to help humanity. Look at the disharmony that's been created." But it was those who persecuted him that created the problems—*his actions* weren't creating the disharmony.

If, however, what you're doing is producing the disharmony, then you should question your intuition. When considering others' reactions, remember, too, that some people's opinions are worth more than others. Watch most closely the reactions of those with clear, impartial minds. You may have the whole world on your side, but if someone whose wisdom you trust doesn't support what you're doing, then you should re-examine your guidance.

I remember an incident from my own life in which disharmony played a role in determining what guidance to follow. My spiritual teacher, Paramhansa Yogananda, was planning to take a small group of us on a trip to India, but told us not to speak about the plans to anyone. Another disciple, who wasn't part of the group going, managed to trick me into thinking that he already knew about it, although he only suspected. Pulling me aside, he said, "Oh, yes, I know all about the trip."

"Well, if you already know," I replied, and began discussing the plans with him.

The man became quite upset and went to Yogananda complaining, "How can you leave me when my health is so poor?" Because of the disharmony created, Yogananda cancelled the trip. He told us, "I was praying for a sign about whether or not we should go to India. When he came to me so upset, I realized now that we can't go." Earlier Yogananda had said to us, "Not until I've set foot on that boat will I believe that I'm going," meaning that he wasn't sure it was meant to happen, but was waiting for a sign. This sign came in the form of the disharmony that was created. (If you're interested in reading more about Yogananda's life, I recommend my book *The Path—One Man's Quest on the Only Path There Is* available from Crystal Clarity Publishers.)

Some Signs Are Strictly Individual

Some signs to follow for guidance are particular to individuals. A highly intuitive woman I knew told me that every time one of her relatives had died, a bird would fly against the window and try to get in. That kind of thing doesn't happen to most of us, but it was true for her. The world tends to reflect back the kind of expectations that we've built up.

Once I was visiting some friends in Sedona, Arizona, and an Apache Indian woman was also a guest at their home at this time. As we were gathered talking, I noticed that she was sitting quietly in a corner holding a lighted match. We were absorbed in our conversation, and I didn't pay much attention to what she was doing. Finally she said, "I'll tell you one thing, you have a lot of will power—too damned much will power."

She had been testing my will power by a peculiar method that worked for her. Using her will, she had been trying to make the match flame go towards me, which she was usually able to do with people. But without my even being aware of what she was doing, the flame kept coming back toward her. For her this was a means of getting insight into another person.

It's fascinating how different signs work for different

people. Try to become aware of outward signs that may be guiding you, and test them to see if they repeatedly prove true over time. These can be your personal tools for receiving guidance.

Look to Tradition

It's also important to hold our intuition up to the light of tradition and honor those realities that have always proved true. We can't create a new set of truths to guide our behavior. How foolish it would be to think, "Lying is in fashion now, so I've decided to become dishonest." Often people do things simply because they're accepted as popular at a certain time. Many of society's changes come about because people vote them in, but you can't vote truth in or out: it simply is, and it doesn't ever change.

Those people who allow themselves to go with fads are unlikely to get true guidance, because they're too much in the habit of going along with the general consensus. Gradually they lose sight of the importance of stepping back from others' opinions and of feeling for themselves what is true. It isn't that we should ignore what others say, but still we need some way of gauging if there's truth in it. Consulting our own intuition best does this.

Throughout my life people have always considered me a maverick, though I've never thought of myself in that way. It's true that I usually don't accept things just because some authority has said so, but I need to feel it inside as well. Actually I'm very traditional, but with regard to lasting principles not passing trends.

We need to uphold tradition in this sense: those people throughout history who have found the truth have experienced the same reality, and they've never disagreed about it. Nobody has ever come along and said, "In this century God isn't love—God is hate." So when you're trying to decide if your guidance is right, ask yourself, "What have people of wisdom done?" It's not enough to follow somebody just because they're a minister, or a scholar, or the president. But consider who said it and ask, "Do they have wisdom? Is this what's been done down through the ages?" If so, then don't think you can get away by doing the opposite.

We can't expect to find some new truth that no else has found, because that's not possible. You may find new phenomenon, but the same basic truths will appear, perhaps differently garbed, whenever people get in tune with their own higher selves. If your guidance is not in tune with wisdom that has proved itself over time, then it's at least reasonable to question it.

Finally, when you test your feelings to see if your guidance rings true, understand that this is a feeling that doesn't change with outward circumstances. It isn't dependent on external things but is centered in your inner self. The happiness you feel when you're in tune with superconsciousness comes not because you've decided to do this or that, but simply because you're centered in the joy of your own self.

CHAPTER FOUR

❖

The Art of Following Your Intuition

Superconsciousness is a part of our own higher self and that of all beings. It's an intelligent force that operates through the consciousness of all, and yet responds to the thoughts of each individual. In drawing true guidance, we need to understand that intuition is a constantly evolving, fluid state of awareness that's always adapting to meet our present needs. It's a subtle flow that needs to be followed in the manner of a surfer riding a wave. Don't think of tuning in to intuition as receiving answers from some prophetic voice from on high, but rather as listening sensitively to the whispers of your own higher self.

Be Willing to Act

Here are some key points that will help you in following your intuition for the best results. First we need to have courage to act on the guidance we receive. As you do this, you'll create a flow of energy that increasingly opens up the doorway to superconsciousness. And if you *continue* to act on your guidance, you'll reach a point where you're using your intuition all the time though you may not be aware of it.

Unfortunately what often happens is that people are afraid to act until they've received a definite confirmation that their guidance is absolutely correct. This hesitancy tends to block the flow of intuition, and the guidance may eventually dry up. Acting on intuition is like drawing water from a natural spring. The more you keep using it, the larger the channel becomes, and the more abundant the flow of water will be.

Paramhansa Yogananda gave a powerful affirmation to help us develop the courage to act on our inner guidance. He said to mentally repeat these words throughout the day: "I will reason, I will will, and I will act, but guide my reason, will, and activity to the right path in everything." This affirmation helps strengthen our understanding that drawing intuitive guidance is a cooperative effort: we must be willing to act, but with the realization that a higher consciousness is working with us and guiding our efforts.

There's a beautiful story from the life of St. Francis of Assisi about having the courage to follow guidance. When Francis was a young man in the little town of Assisi, Italy, he began to feel an inward call to follow the example of Christ. One day he knelt in prayer in the crumbling chapel of San Damiano, which was little more than a pile of ruins, and asked Jesus to give him guidance for his life. As he prayed with deep sincerity before a large painted crucifix, the image of Christ on the cross became real and appeared before him saying, "Francis, rebuild my church, which as you can see has fallen into ruin." This was a time in the history of Christianity when the church had become corrupt, and the majority of Christians had lost their faith and devotion for God.

Poor Francis was amazed by these words! Because he was kneeling in the crumbling chapel, he thought Christ literally meant that he was to rebuild that little church. So Francis began the backbreaking labor of rebuilding San Damiano alone. In the cold of winter he hauled large stones to the site, and one by one put them into place. Gradually the chapel of San Damiano began to take shape again.

The young men of Assisi started to notice what Francis was doing, and though some mocked him, a few were moved by his joy and determination. They joined him in his efforts, and together they rebuilt the chapel that still stands today, some seven hundred years later. More than just rebuilding San Damiano, St. Francis had begun to rebuild Christ's "real church" by bringing a simple, living faith back to the people of his time and starting a rebirth of true Christianity.

We can ask, "Why didn't Jesus tell him what he really wanted from the beginning?" By *acting* on the guidance, even if he misunderstood it, St. Francis started the flow of his intuition which grew stronger over time.

Don't wait for some sort of pronouncement, or expect a vision or voice from the clouds, but have the courage to act. By *not* acting, we often close the door to real guidance, whereas in the process of acting, the energy begins to flow more clearly. And don't worry too much about making mistakes. If you have a courageous attitude, you'll find that even if you haven't taken the best course of action at first, over time your guidance will be clarified. Eventually you may realize that though you totally went off in the wrong direction, things have somehow turned out much better than if you'd started off right in the first place.

Guidance Can Come in Unexpected Ways

Superconscious guidance may come in ways that won't always be under your control, but because you've asked for it, the guidance will begin to lead you. When you get in tune with an intuitive flow, events seem to happen almost automatically that move you in the right direction.

When you're really trying to follow inner guidance the superconscious will help you in marvelous ways. There's a wonderful story illustrating this point that happened in the early phases of a spiritual community called Ananda that I founded. (A more complete account of this community is in my book, *A Place Called Ananda*, available from Crystal Clarity Publishers.) We were designing and constructing one of our first major buildings that would set the aesthetic tone for the development of the rest of the community. The new building was sited on a large hill that was a visual focus for the property. Intuitively I felt that the Publications Building, as it was to be called, needed a sweeping, soaring look to create the impression of a bird in flight. Although I worked with several architects, none of them was able to capture the subtle lines of the design I had in mind.

With no other options available I decided to take

matters into my own hands. Putting forth a lot of will power, I tried clearly to visualize a building that would reflect the soaring energy I felt was right. Suddenly the image of a beautiful structure came into my mind, and I quickly drew it on a small slip of paper.

Later that day I handed the little drawing to the foreman of our construction crew, and asked him, "Can you build this?" He was more than a little surprised by my request. The design was an unusual one with a double curve, both outward and upward, to the sweeping line of the roof. After studying the drawing, he summoned up his courage and said, "I've never done anything like this before, but let's give it a try."

At first the work on the building was straightforward and easy, and it went up quickly. Then as the work on the roof began, the foreman would spend long hours every night trying to figure out how to direct his crew the next day. He would ask for guidance as to how to do the next phase, and he was shown, but only as far as the next day's work was concerned.

Finally the day came when he no longer knew how

to proceed. The carpenters showed up, did a few peripheral jobs, then the whole project seemed to have reached an impasse. To keep some energy going, the foreman said, "Well, I guess there's nothing left to do but clean up the site, and put away our tools."

At this point a car pulled up, and a stranger got out. "What are you fellows working on here?" he asked pleasantly. The foreman talked with him a bit, and then began showing him the plans for the building. He explained that we were stumped as to how to create the double curve of the roof. The man paused and seemed very thoughtful. "This is very strange," he said. "I'm an engineer and probably one of the few men around who specializes in this kind of construction. I live about five hundred miles from here, but for some reason this morning I had the feeling to drive up to this area and look around."

To our amazement, he began giving us the practical advice we needed to finish the work. The completed building was beautiful, and it stands today as a testimony to the power of the superconscious to help those who have the courage to follow it against all odds.

Don't Be Discouraged by Obstacles

At first when you're trying to follow your guidance you may run up against blocks and obstructions. If you've built up a certain amount of energy in terms of mental and emotional patterns in the one direction, those patterns will act as a psychic wall blocking your efforts to move in another direction. You may think, "I guess I'm not supposed to do this," but the obstacles may be there only to test you. A friend told me an amusing story related to this. He was an older man, and he and his wife had attended a concert one evening at a local church. As they were coming out, he fell on the steps and broke his arm. Later he told me, "The moral of that obviously is never go to church."

Many people reason this way: When they're trying to follow intuition, and they're met with obstacles, they conclude they're not meant to do it. But it's important to keep in mind that if you're sincerely asking for guidance, and inwardly feeing what you're doing is right, then you should look at the obstacles as challenges to your will power. As Paramhansa Yogananda said, "There are no obstacles, only opportunities." Try to see the blocks in your path as opportunities for you to put out more energy toward the accomplishment of your goals.

Listen Each Step of the Way

Remember also to balance the courage to act with a constant effort to offer your guidance up for correction. Never presume that you're absolutely correct for the entire course of your actions. If you begin to feel too sure about a thing, you may streak for the horizon, whereas your intuition was only telling you to go to the next corner and turn right. Continually hold your feelings of guidance up for further refinement, and you'll eventually reach the point where you know when to veer off from your initial course. It's easy to make mistakes, but if you remain humble and avoid being presumptuous about your guidance, you'll be able to tune in to the superconscious level.

Another point is that if you *don't* feel any clear guidance, try a little bit tentatively, but don't do too much. One of the biggest mistakes I made in my life happened when I wasn't feeling clear guidance, but thought, "All right, I'll just go with full force." The resulting events brought me a great deal of suffering. Even though my actions were done with good will, I had to admit to myself later that I didn't really feel guidance. I merely felt that my common sense told me to do it, and I went for the horizon.

So if you don't feel strong clarity, don't go all out. Try, but always with a sufficient degree of sensitivity and tentativeness. Then when real guidance does come, you'll be able to recognize it. Take one step at a time, but if it's not feeling right, don't take too many. Too many people leap off the diving board before checking to see if it's the day the pool is emptied.

Apply the Test of Common Sense

In working with intuition, don't ignore the simple dictates of your own good judgment. Sometimes truth *will* defy common sense, but it would be foolish to disregard it entirely. The mind is capable of many games, and it's risky to trust it completely, but the universe is governed by laws that need to be observed. If your guidance tells you to jump off a cliff, use your common sense and obey the law of gravity until further notice.

It's like the story of the student who was told by his spiritual teacher that God is in everything. One day he was walking down a jungle lane when he heard just ahead the crashing of a rogue elephant out of control. By the uproar, the man could tell that the elephant was headed straight in his direction. The driver, clinging for dear life to the elephant's back, was shouting to everyone, "Get out of the way! Get out of the way! Mad elephant!" The man thought, "My teacher said that God is in everything. Therefore, God is in the elephant, and

God is in me. How can God hurt God?" So he just stood there as the elephant charged up to him.

Picking him up in his trunk, the elephant threw the man to the side, and nearly killed him. The man was finally able to drag himself to his teacher, and said, "Look what happened! Your teaching is wrong." The teacher replied, "What do you mean?" He explained, "Well, I reasoned that if God is in everything, then He's in the elephant and in me. So how could God hurt God?" The teacher said, "This is true, but why didn't you listen to God in the form of the driver who was shouting at you to get out of the way?"

Working With Others

When working with others on a project, it's better to state your intuition tentatively. In other words, don't try to persuade people just because you've had the guidance to do something. They need to have their own guidance too. I may intuitively feel something very strongly, but will state it conditionally with words like: "It makes sense, doesn't it?" or "It seems like a good idea. Maybe we should try it." I usually put it that way, even though I rarely do anything unless I've first felt it inwardly.

If you want to involve people in what you're doing, let them be in a position to arrive at an understanding in their own way. Let sweet reason be it's own argument, rather than any claim of intuition. This approach produces much greater harmony in human relations. Even if you feel it's really true—even if it *is* really true—if it's meant to work, it will work. The people who make a big commotion about their guidance are usually those who lack true inner clarity.

Another reason for not talking too much to others about your intuitive feelings is that we need to have a healthy respect for the possibility of error. If we're always talking about our inner guidance, others will develop a certain expectation about our accuracy, even though we may know that we're not always right. There was a time, for example, when couples I knew who were about to have a baby would ask me to tell them the sex of their child. I didn't have any expectation that anybody would believe me one way or the other, so I said what I felt.

After about twelve times, my friends began to notice that I had always been right—so they expected me to be right continually. I thought, "I don't want this expectation, because I'm not sure from what level I'm feeling this intuition. It could just be my imagination, and I could make a mistake. What if they've already bought clothes for a boy, and it turns out to be a girl?" So from then on, I've refused to say anything about the subject, because I didn't want to get boxed in by people's expectations.

When you talk about your intuitions too much, you tend to lose them. In working with others, share your inner guidance as a possible alternative rather than an absolute. By keeping it inside, your guidance over time will grow stronger.

Too Many Objections Can Block the Flow

We've talked about the importance of getting input from others to test our guidance, but you'll find difficulty if you move too much in this direction. It's been my experience that when I'm trying to launch some project, people will inevitably come in with objections. There's a time at the beginning of a project when objections are good, but after a certain point they only pull the mind down into problem consciousness. Voicing objections is a part of the act of discrimination, and there's a time and place for that, but the "no-saying" principle cannot give real guidance, unless it also comes up with solutions.

How many times throughout history have great scientists had to persevere over the objections of others, because they believed in the truth of their intuition. When Thomas Edison was trying to find the right material to use as a filament for the light bulb, many people raised objections and said it couldn't be done. He persevered for years against the advice of the "nay-sayers," because he knew inwardly it was possible. After experimenting with over a thousand different filaments, he tried tungsten, and this was the solution he'd been searching for. Through the strength of his inner conviction, Edison was able to give electric light to the world.

*　　*　　*　　*　　*

Remember these principles: Even if our actions are going in the wrong direction, if we've sincerely asked for inner guidance, we will be redirected in the right course to take. To attune ourselves to the flow of superconsciousness, we must live in a way that expresses courage and determination. And we must balance our efforts with humility and openness to all.

CHAPTER FIVE

❖

How to Recognize False Guidance

We've been talking thus far about techniques and attitudes that will help us to tune in to true guidance, but there are also pitfalls that we need to watch out for. These are the false guides that seem to offer us direction and clarity, but in the end only lead us into greater doubt and confusion.

One of the big traps we can fall into is to allow the desires of the ego, our likes and dislikes, to influence and distort our intuition. Paramhansa Yogananda defined the ego as the soul identified with the body and the personality. The ordinary human being lives primarily in ego, not soul, awareness. He identifies himself with his body type, facial characteristics, or mental and emotional traits, and loses awareness of his superconscious potential. Though knowledge of our soul nature always remains on some level, we forget our more expanded reality and allow ourselves to remain in the limited consciousness of the ego.

How Egoic Desires Create Delusion

Let's discuss now how the ego operates, and how it can mislead us in our search for guidance. The Indian scriptures identify four aspects of consciousness: *mon, buddhi, ahankara,* and *chitta. Mon* means mind, *buddhi* is intellect, *ahankara* is ego-consciousness, and *chitta* is the feelings of the heart, the likes and dislikes.

To better understand how these aspects of consciousness work, we can use the illustration that Paramhansa Yogananda gave of the image of a horse reflected in a pool of water. At first the mind, or *mon*, just observes the image of the horse, and sees it as a reflection. The mind reflects to the consciousness whatever it experiences through the senses, while the intellect divides and defines it. The intellect, or *buddhi*, then says, "This is a horse. That is a tree. And that over there is a human being." The analytical process of the intellect separates the world around us into fragments, and we lose sight of the underlying unity behind it all.

Next the ego, or *ahankara*, steps in and divides the world into "mine" and "not mine." It says, "That's *my* horse." This is the beginning of the process of distortion of reality, but it's not yet the final stage. We're not necessarily caught in delusion merely by the thought of the reflection being *our* horse, because we can take responsibility for many things in our lives—our family, home, or job—and not be personally attached to them.

The problem comes with the emotional reactions of the heart, the *chitta*. It says, "How *happy* I am to see my horse!" Suddenly like a gust of wind over that pond, our reactions distort the whole thing. What before was merely a horse, now becomes either a beautiful horse, or a very special horse, or perhaps an old tired horse that we'd like to replace with a *better* horse. The reactive processes of the heart, our likes and dislikes, amplify the thought of "I" and "mine," and make us happy or miserable depending on our responses. This is how our real delusions begin, and how we can be misled from receiving true guidance.

In this analysis of the different aspects of consciousness, the mind merely reflects, the intellect dissects, the ego makes a personal identification, but finally it's the emotions that create the ripples of feeling. These distort the calm surface of the water of our impartial judgment. Never trust your guidance when there's any personal feeling involved in it, because you can't be sure from what level of consciousness it's coming. In fact, let's put it further: you can be *sure* that your guidance is wrong when you're too emotionally involved, because your desires have interfered with your ability to be clear and objective.

Many times I've seen that what people consider to

be intuition is really only the projected desires of the heart, because they want things to come out in a certain way. They'll think, "Please show me the right choice to make here. But it's *this* one, okay? Okay!" The powerful emotional energy of our likes and dislikes is a strong force in overriding real intuition.

Remember that the basic technique for drawing intuition is to project your question strongly at the point between the eyebrows, and then calmly try to feel the response in your heart. If the heart's feelings are already biased by personal desires, then the outcome is predetermined. It's like being in a court of law and asking for a fair and impartial decision from a judge who's already been bribed against you.

That's why it's so important to be able to recognize the feelings of calmness and impartiality that are unmistakable signs of real guidance. Otherwise, it's like the man who went to a store to buy a green suit. The salesman knew they didn't have any green ones, so he gave him a gray one instead saying, "If you want a green suit, come stand under the green light." We can convince ourselves that our guidance is true according to how we color it with our desires.

The False Guide of the Subconscious

The subconscious mind also can masquerade as a source of true guidance. If you allow yourself to be influenced by the subconscious, you'll experience a kind of reality, but it will prove false and misleading, like the cloudy, distorted images in a dream. Some of our dreams can seem very real, but the real test comes when we try to integrate our subconscious experiences with the objective world around us. They never quite match up. One sign of insanity is to become so convinced that our subjective impressions are real that we can't relate to the reality of others.

One of the foremost exponents of the science of yoga, Patanjali, who's been the recognized authority on the subject for thousands of years, states that "false visions" are one of the major obstacles to tuning into superconsciousness. We must keep the mind concentrated and energetic when asking for guidance, because a passive mind will be overly receptive to subconscious images. Just beneath our conscious awareness, the subconscious mind is constantly conjuring up impressions that have no reasonable basis.

People may imagine they detect malice in an innocuous statement, or the certainty of failure in a temporary setback. They may see visions and be convinced that they're real, but such images aren't necessarily superconscious phenomena: they can be merely hallucinations.

Somebody once told me that he'd had a vision of Jesus Christ coming to him in the flesh. I asked him, "What did he do?" "Well, we sat down and had a cigarette together," he answered. The subconscious mind can do extraordinary things, because obviously such a great soul would not appear just to have a smoke with someone.

Paramhansa Yogananda told us about a man who came to him and claimed that he could go into superconsciousness and astrally travel all over the world.

Yogananda intuitively knew that it wasn't true, but he also wanted to help the man, so he didn't denounce his claims. He invited him up to his hotel room and said, "Now go into superconsciousness, and tell me what you see."

As the man sat there, Yogananda could see that his eyes and his whole body were restless and fidgety. It's impossible to go into superconsciousness if you can't even control your body. After a while, the man couldn't stand the wait any longer, and he blurted out, "Why don't you ask me where I am?" Calmly Yogananda asked him, "Well, where are you?" He replied in a deep vibrating voice, "I'm on top of the dome of the Taj Mahal!" Somewhat amused, Yogananda said, "There must be something the matter with your own dome. I see you sitting right here in my room."

"All right, all right. Test me again," he said. Then Yogananda suggested, "Well, if you can go to the Taj Mahal, then you can certainly go downstairs. Why don't you use your powers to go down to the restaurant in this hotel, and tell me what you see?" So the man did, or imagined he did, and described a few things in the restaurant. He was sincere, but just had a very vivid imagination.

Yogananda, who did have the power of seeing things at a distance, then described the restaurant as *he* saw it. Immediately they both went down together to find out who was right. They found the restaurant was clearly the way Yogananda had described it, and not at all the way he had said. The man was greatly humbled, and in this way Yogananda was able to help him break the habit of accepting subconscious images as real.

Another person I knew imagined that he was hearing voices from higher spiritual realms. These voices would say to him, "Aren't you glad you're you?" He would reply, "Yes, yes, yes! I'm very glad I'm me!" At first I was open to the possibility that the voices were from a higher source. After all, people throughout history, Joan of Arc for example, have been guided by heavenly voices.

Over time as I observed him, however, I noticed that the more he accepted these voices the more he demonstrated negative attitudes. He became increasingly arrogant and self-centered, because these subconscious voices were only feeding his ego. If you're acting in attunement with superconscious guidance, you'll find yourself becoming filled with positive qualities like humility and inner joy. It was a sad case, and in the end those voices ruined his life.

The Trap of Superstition

Another harmful result of mental passivity is that we read too much meaning into outward signs. I used to know a couple of sisters who were practically incapable of doing anything because they were so superstitious. They might have the intention of going downtown, then one of them would trip over the corner of a rug, and they'd take this as a sign that they weren't meant to go.

Many people use such trivial signs to guide their actions. Every culture also builds up its own superstitions over time that become accepted as realities. We've all seen people following the superstition of throwing salt over their left shoulder to ward off evil spirits if they've accidentally knocked over a saltshaker. Who knows the origins of such superstitions? But it's important to develop our own inner clarity and not become too influenced by superstitious beliefs.

Sometimes inexplicable things do happen that may have some inner meaning. In the community I founded, the first land we purchased was in a beautiful wooded area in the Sierra Nevada foothills, and was to be developed for a meditation retreat. When we began bringing in materials and equipment for construction of the first buildings, large trees kept falling over for no apparent reason blocking the only access road into the property.

It seemed as if the forces of nature were trying to prevent us from moving onto the land. If we had been superstitious, we could have taken this as a bad omen. But undeterred, we carried on with the project. Moving the fallen trees aside and trying to work sensitively with the natural beauty of the land, we constructed a meditation temple and other buildings.

The Meditation Retreat drew many guests for nearly ten years, and then we decided to move it to another part of our property where we could develop more facilities for our visitors. The original Retreat was left as a place for guests to take seclusion, which would involve less activity. As we began moving things to the new Retreat, the same phenomenon happened, but this time in reverse. Large trees again began to fall blocking the road, but now it seemed that the nature forces were happy to have us there, and were trying to stop us from leaving.

This world is a great deal more curious than we may realize. The safest thing to do with regard to interpreting things as meaningful signs is to see it as a game, and don't take them too seriously. Let a sign of guidance be very strong before you act on it, and don't allow yourself to become superstitious about little things

Should We Depend on Psychics?

Many people go to psychics to get readings about their past lives or to foretell future events, but we need to be cautious about whether they really have the abilities they claim. The question that we should ask is, "Was the psychic able to access a true superconscious state?" I read a book recently that evaluated the accuracy of different well-known psychics, who are quoted annually in supermarket tabloids for their predictions about the coming year. According to this book, one prediction out of a hundred actually came true.

After reading the book, I decided to do my own private research about the accuracy of a well-known woman psychic. I thought, "She's got a good reputation for seeing the future, but I'm going to write down what she says to see what actually happens." Over a period of time, I observed that her predictions were no more accurate than if I'd asked a five-year old child what he thought was going to happen.

Some psychics build their reputation on the fact that they make so *many* predictions. If you say enough things, some of them are bound to come true. But all too often, they'll say, "Aha! I was right because I predicted that such and such would happen," and they conveniently forget to mention all the things that didn't come to pass.

Certainly there are men and women of true super-conscious vision. My spiritual teacher, Paramhansa Yogananda, proved to us time and again that he could both read our thoughts (often to our embarrassment) and see future events. But he did it in such a humble, under-stated way that often you had to think about what he'd said to realize the depth of his consciousness.

A person of true vision will never allow you to de-pend too much on him. If he's wise, he'll help you to de-velop your own intuition through the use of your will power rather than passively depending on him. I've often seen that people who go to psychics become de-pendent on them for every little thing. If they lose a handkerchief, they'll run to the psychic to find it for them.

In India, many years ago, I had a fascinating experi-ence with predictions for the future. Some friends took me to a little village in the state of Punjab where there was a segment of a very ancient manuscript called the

Book of Bhrigu, supposedly written thousands of years ago by a great visionary named Bhrigu. This manuscript was reputed to have predictions about the lives of people who would live in the future, people who were alive today. The *pundit*, or scholar, who read the book didn't know me, and yet there was a page that had my spiritual name, Kriyananda, written on it. It said that I was born in Rumania, and that I was a writer and teacher. There were many details, beyond what this scholar could have possibly known, that were quite accurate.

It said, for example, that my father had named me James. Because I usually go by my middle name, Donald, most people don't know that James is my first name. The only way the pundit could have known this would have been to go to the Home Ministry in Rumania and find it there. The possibility of this Indian pundit leaving his remote village to check with the Rumanian Ministry about my true surname seemed, at best, to be highly unlikely.

The reading also said that I grew up in America and that Yogananda was my spiritual teacher. It went on to say that I had two brothers, but that no living sister was possible, though one would die in my mother's womb. I'd never known that my mother had suffered a miscarriage, but when I got back to America, I asked her about this, and she confirmed it.

The pundit also said that I would return to America within two months, although at the time I didn't have any plans to return. And, in fact, I did have to return home unexpectedly the following month. At the end of my page, there were predictions for my future that have come true for the most part.

Naturally, I was fascinated by all this, but wanted to make sure it wasn't a hoax. I took my page to the Indian National Archives Laboratory, and asked them, "Can you tell me how old this page is?" I thought perhaps they could do a carbon-14 dating on it to determine the age, but they weren't set up for that process. Then I asked, "Can you at least tell me if it was written recently?" They replied, "How recently?" I thought, "Well, I've known this pundit for only two days," so I asked, "Within the past month?"

They replied, "Well, that's easy to tell. The ink will set in a page over a period of time so that it can't be washed away." They took a wet cloth and tried to wipe away some of the writing, but the ink was deeply set into the page. "We can't say how old it is exactly, but it's definitely older than a month," they told me.

Then I took the page to the director of the National Archeological Institute and asked him if he could tell how old the page was. After looking at it, he said, "It's not very old." He was used to working with very ancient manuscripts, some from five thousand years ago. This page was, in fact, supposed to be a copy of the original that is reputedly buried somewhere in Tibet. Pursuing the question, I asked, "How old would you say?" He looked at the page again and said, "It's only about one hundred and fifty years old." That was old enough to impress me.

Some things that the book said about my life thus far

turned out to be true, though I didn't know about them at that time. Other things it predicted for the future seemed impossible to actually happen, and yet they came to pass. It was an amazing experience. Yet unfortunately I found that many people would go to this book for guidance about everything, and for them it became just another psychic phenomenon. The benefit of guidance from a true visionary is that it can give us the magnetism to draw intuition from our own superconsciousness. We miss the point if we become dependent on them.

*   *   *   *   *

In developing the ability to draw true guidance, we want to gain *experience*, not have *experiences*. We want to acquire the kind of experience that helps us recognize real intuition. The false guides of egoic desires and the subconscious cloud our intuition by drawing us into too much self-involvement. True guidance can never be found if there is too much focus on a sense of

"I" and "mine." Relying on superstition and psychics can weaken our will and dry up the flow of energy from the superconscious. Only by raising our consciousness and exerting dynamic energy, can we achieve that state of expansive awareness where true guidance can be found.

CHAPTER SIX

❖

Meditation—
The Doorway To
Superconscious
Guidance

The more you seek to be guided by intuition, the stronger its flow will be in your life, and the greater success you'll achieve in every undertaking. For the rational mind can only point to probable solutions. Intuition, rooted as it is in superconsciousness, will supply you with clear answers.

From a superconscious perspective, all life is a

unity. From a rational perspective, life is a *disunity*—a bewildering jigsaw puzzle, often, with many pieces that never seem to belong together. To superconsciousness, everything is related. Not relative, merely: *related*. You don't have to be in superconsciousness to *think* superconsciously. All you have to do is train your mind to adjust your thinking to superconscious modes of perception.

Think more unitively, less analytically. Concentrate on finding the relationships between things; don't dwell at length on the differences. See others as your own greater Self. They are not alien to you. Look on them as friends, even if they appear outwardly to be strangers. The more we feel we are a part of a greater reality, the more readily we can access the realms of intuition, because we realize that they're a part of our own higher nature.

Basic Principles for Drawing Inner Guidance

Let's review the main points we've covered:

1) Ask for guidance from superconsciousness at the point between the eyebrows.

2) Wait for a response in the heart center. Be completely impartial. Don't intrude your personal desires into this process.

3) If no guidance comes, pose several alternative solutions. See if one of them receives special endorsement in the heart.

4) Guidance often comes only after an idea has been made concrete by setting it in motion. If, therefore, you receive no answer, act in whatever way seems reasonable to you, but continue to listen for guidance in the heart. At a certain point, if your direction is right, you will feel the endorsement you've been seeking. But if your direction is wrong, suddenly you will *know* it's wrong. In that

case, try something else, until the endorsement comes.

5) To refuse to act until you receive inner guidance is good only if you can keep your level of energy and expectation high. For it's high energy and high expectation that attract guidance. If you must act because you have no other way of maintaining that level of energy, then go ahead and act. Often it is better to act, even in error, than not to act at all.

6) Even if you feel inner guidance, never presume on it. That guidance may tell you, metaphorically speaking, to go north, but if you cease listening you may not hear it when, at the next corner, it tells you to turn east.

7) Never use the claim of inner guidance as an argument for convincing others to listen to you. The flow of superconsciousness is always humble, never boastful. It doesn't cooperate with attitudes that discourage others from seeking their own inner guidance.

Meditation and Superconsciousness

We all get glimpses of superconsciousness in our daily life, but deep perceptions of it can really only come to us in the deep stillness of meditation. Properly speaking, meditation truly begins once the thoughts and emotions have been stilled. It's a state of intense inward awareness, a state in which one's attention is no longer engaged in the outward activities of our lives, but is wholly engrossed in the superconscious experience. Meditation may be loosely defined as any practice of which the goal *is* superconsciousness. It's the process of retraining our awareness to operate not from the conscious or subconscious level, but from the superconscious.

The essential attitude for correct meditation is one of *listening.* The mind must be kept *receptive,* because we can't think our way into deep meditation. Nor, indeed, can you think your way to true guidance and inspiration. You can only receive wisdom: you cannot concoct it. A truth must be perceived in that calm awareness which is superconsciousness.

Meditation, then, is not creating answers: It is perceiving, or receiving them. And this is the secret of true guidance.

As we've said, meditation is listening. Most people seldom listen. They're like out-of-tune musical instruments. Because they no longer are able to tune into their own essential nature, their interactions with life and other people produce only discords. They are deaf to the symphony of sounds in the world around them. They are deaf to other people, for they are more interested in speaking their own minds. They behave as though perpetually campaigning for their own ideas. Like bettors at a horse race, they keep *willing* the "right" horse to win.

To understand what meditation is we must learn to listen to what *is*, and not keep insisting on what we think it *ought* to be. We must try to tune in to things as they are. Meditation is the opposite of imposing your will on the world. Try to relinquish, even for just a few minutes, the process of concocting plans and projects for the future. Be more, not less, conscious, however.

Superconsciousness is a state of dynamic awareness. Many people have had glimpses of this state during moments of inner stillness, or during sleep. Meditation is a means of attuning the mind to superconsciousness, and eventually entering that state. All that is needed to reach that level of awareness is to disperse the fog of mental restlessness. In meditation, by gazing upward to the point between the eyebrows in a state of deep calmness and relaxation, you will become fully aware, in time, of that highest aspect of your being.

We've spoken of the importance of the attitude of receptivity in meditation. The more deeply and consciously receptive you become, the deeper and more satisfying will your meditation be. By receptivity, you will begin to understand your connection with all Life. For we are like ripples on the great ocean of existence. Our appearance of separateness is an illusion, merely, produced by ego-consciousness, and reinforced by our attachment to little preoccupations.

We are far more than the individual life dramas we find ourselves in. In our greater reality, we are the ocean of life itself. By receptivity of feeling and sympathy, as well as thought, you will develop intuition, the hallmark of superconsciousness.

How Do We Practice Meditation?

Meditation is a state of intense awareness achieved by stilling and concentrating the thought. It's a journey to the center of our being, a process so perfectly natural that we don't have to learn how to meditate. Rather, we have to unlearn those habits and attitudes that keep us from experiencing our natural state of expanded awareness. We simply need to still the mental restlessness which, like static on a radio, prevents us from hearing clearly our own natural "program." Deeper states of meditation come automatically as we peel away the layers of tension and attachments that prevent us from being more aware.

To learn more in-depth about the art and science of meditation, I recommend that you read *Meditation for Starters* and *How to Meditate* available from Crystal Clarity Publishers. Here are some practical hints to get you started in meditation:

1) **Regularity**: Set aside the same time or times each day for your meditation. Recommended times are dawn (or just after awakening), high noon, twilight, and midnight (or just before bedtime.) It's best to meditate on an empty stomach or two to three hours after eating a large meal.

2) **Exercise**: If you have time, exercise a little before meditation to awaken your energy and to release any tension. Yoga postures are excellent for this. Paramhansa Yogananda developed a wonderful series of exercises for drawing energy into the body at will that he called Energization Exercises. You can learn more about them in *Lessons in Meditation* from Crystal Clarity Publishers. Remember that the exercises one does before meditation should calm and relax, not excite, the nervous system.

3) **Location**: Set aside a room, or small part of a room just for meditation. Try to find the quietest spot possible, or if this is difficult, try using comfortable foam earplugs or headphones to block out noise. Be sure the room isn't stuffy and is a bit on the cool side with good ventilation. Have a comfortable place to sit. Some people like to set up a small simple altar as focal point with pictures, flowers, and a candle. You'll find that the vibrations of meditation will build in this space. Sit facing east if possible. Yogis say that there are certain natural currents that flow from east to west which help us to meditate better. North is also a good direction.

4) **Posture**: Sit erect! It's fine to sit on a chair or in a comfortable cross-legged position on the floor or using cushions. If you sit in a chair, don't lean against the back of the chair. Meditation benches are helpful, too. Whatever your position, keep your back straight, chest raised, head erect, eyes closed, and hands resting with the palms up-

turned on your lap, preferably at the juncture of the thighs and the abdomen. Yogis also recommend that you cover your meditation seat with a natural fiber cloth like a wool or silk blanket. They say this protects us from the downward pull of earth currents.

5) **Length of time**: Don't set unrealistic goals for yourself. It's better to meditate five or ten minutes and be consistent about it, than to overreach yourself, build up mental resistance, and meditate irregularly. You can gradually increase your length of meditation, as you feel comfortable. It's also helpful to try to have one longer meditation each week, and to meditate with other people, especially those who have been meditating longer than you. The energy of a group meditation often helps you to meditate longer than you would ordinarily be able to on your own.

6) **To begin**: Some people find it helpful to do a mental prayer for guidance in their meditation practice. You can start with some breathing exer-

cises. Inhale, tense the whole body, then throw the breath out and relax. Do this two or three times. Now do some Regular Breathing techniques: Inhale to a certain count, hold the breath for that same count, and then exhale to the same count. The count can be 8-8-8, 10-10-10, 12-12-12, or whatever you feel comfortable with. Do this six to twelve times. Then inhale, tense the whole body one last time, and throw the breath out and relax the body completely.

7) **Hold the body still**: You should feel relaxed now, but try to refrain from any restless movements. Mentally check from time to time to see if any body part has inadvertently become tensed again. Feel a sense of space and an awareness of freedom from body-awareness.

8) **Concentrate at the point between the eyebrows**: As we've said, this is the seat of superconsciousness, and it's sometimes referred to as the Spiritual Eye. When you concentrate at this point, try to do so without any mental or phys-

ical tension. We simply want to make the Spiritual Eye the one-pointed focus of our attention. When our awareness returns to the habitual patterns of thinking, reviewing, and planning that are the activities of the conscious mind, gently and repeatedly return your attention to the point between the eyebrows.

9) **Observe the natural flow of your breath**: Inhale deeply, and then slowly exhale. Wait for the breath to come in of its own accord, and watch its flow. As the breath flows out naturally, again observe the movement. This is not a breathing exercise. Don't inhale and exhale deliberately. Simply *watch* the breath. Don't watch your *body* breathing. Notice the breath itself.

Be particularly aware of the rest points between the breaths. Enjoy the peace, and the feeling of inward release and freedom that you feel when your body is without breath. Practice this technique as long as you feel to.

After a time, as you become more interiorized,

concentrate at the Spiritual Eye. Concentrating here brings the awareness closer to the upper part of the nasal passage, where the breath enters the body. To center the awareness here makes it easier to watch the breath, and at the same time brings it into harmony with spiritual awareness.

10) **Meditate with joy!** Don't wait for joy to come to you, but be joyful first yourself. Meditation simply helps you remember, on ever deepening levels of awareness, who and what you really are!

11) **Ask for inner guidance**: In this calm, joyful state of meditation, we are now ready to practice the technique for drawing intuitive guidance. Send your request out at the Spiritual Eye from the concentrated, uplifted mind, and receive the response in the calm feelings of the heart. After preparing your consciousness in meditation, you'll receive more clearly and quickly true inner guidance.

A Guided Meditation

Imagine a choir composed of every atom in the universe, each one an individual, but all of them singing together in blissful harmony.

In your own mind, join that mighty choir, composed of all life. Determine from today on to sing in harmony with the universe. Don't impose on the great anthem of life your little wishes for how you want the music to sound. Feel how all the notes—the birds, the wind, the flow of water, the laughter in happy minds—join together in a perfect balance and harmony. Unite your notes to that Infinite Sound.

The more you do so, the more deeply you will know yourself to be an expression of the soaring anthem of Infinity: and you will know that you are playing your part well in the great symphony of life.

About the Author

J. Donald Walters is an internationally known author, lecturer, and composer. Widely recognized as one of the world's foremost authorities on meditation, yoga, and spiritual practice, he has taught these principles and techniques to hundreds of thousands of students around the world.

By drawing upon intuitive guidance and spiritual practice, Walters has written more than 80 books on a variety of topics including leadership, education, creativity, and moral values and composed over 300 pieces of music. These books and music have sold over 3 million copies worldwide and been translated into 24 languages. As a composer, Walters is perhaps best known for the top-selling albums *Mystic Harp* and *Mystic Harp* 2, featuring the legendary harpist Derek Bell, of the 5-time Grammy Award-winning group The Chieftains.

Walters is perhaps best known as the founder and spiritual director of the Ananda, a worldwide network of intentional communities. In existence since 1968, Ananda is generally recognized as one of the most successful intentional communities in the world with branches in California, Oregon, Washington, Rhode Island, and Italy.

Index

❖

Decisions
indecision and, 23
influences on, 16–18, 22
intuition and, 24
rational/analytical, 22–23, 82–83, 102
superconscious state and, 24

Desires, 81–86, 98–99

Detachment, 37–42, 48, 61

Disharmony, 56–57

Dreaming, 18–20, 49

Ego
defined, 81–82
delusion from, 82–86
desires of, 81–86, 98–99
emotion and, 40, 82, 83–86
as false guide, 81–86, 98–99

Emotion
desire and, 83–86
identifying with, 82
intuitive guidance and, 40

Energy
blocked, 54
chakras, 30–33, 34–35, 103
intuitive guidance and, 35–36, 87, 99, 104
joy and, 49–50, 61, 90
passivity vs., 87, 90

Energy body. *See* Astral body

Exercises/techniques
ajna chakra, 31–33
anahata chakra, 31–32
intuitive guidance, 34–35
meditation, 108–15
superconscious mind, 27–28

Expectation
impartiality and, 37–42, 77, 84–86
importance of, 36, 104

Experience, 47, 98–99

Eye position, 27–28

False guidance, 81–99
attitudes and, 89–90
ego desires as, 81–86, 98–99
psychics and, 92–98, 99
of subconscious, 49, 86–90
superstition as, 90–92, 99
See also Intuitive guidance

Feelings
calmness, 48–49, 85
clarity of, 48, 49
emotion and, 40, 82, 83–86
inner joy, 49–50, 61, 90, 114
listening and, 38, 54, 72–73
steadfastness of, 48, 61
subtlety of, 46–48

Future predictions, 94–98

Heart chakra. *See* Anahata chakra

Higher self, 63–64, 102

Humility, 79, 90, 104

Idea body. *See* Causal body

Indecision, 23

Influences
decisions and, 16–18, 22
detachment from, 37–42, 48, 61
on others, 75–77, 104
outside, 17–18, 22, 41–42, 78–79
from psychics, 92–98, 99
superstitious, 90–92, 99

Inner joy, 49–50, 61, 90, 114

Intellect (buddhi), 82–83. *See also* Analytical mind

Intuition
chakras and, 30–33
defined, 15
gender of, 16
impersonal nature of, 16, 84–86
individual nature of, 51–54, 57–59
source of, 15, 24
Yogananda, Paramhansa on, 33

Index

About the *for Starters* series

❖

The ". . . *for Starters*" series was created to give both beginning and long-time practitioners a brief yet thorough introduction to some of the most popular spiritual topics and practices of our day. More than mere overviews, the books in this series will help you quickly gain a foothold of understanding—and even more importantly—they will help you find the enthusiasm and energy necessary to incorporate these principles and practices into your daily life. That is, they actively help you get *started*.

Titles in the *"for Starters"* series

Meditation for Starters
J. Donald Walters

Meditation brings balance into our lives, providing an oasis of profound rest and renewal. Doctors are prescribing it for a variety of stress-related diseases. This award-winning book offers simple but powerful guidelines for attaining inner peace. Learn to prepare the body and mind for meditation, special breathing techniques, ways to focus and "let go," develop superconscious awareness, sharpen your willpower, and increase intuition and calmness. Taught by J. Donald Walters, an internationally respected spiritual teacher who has practiced meditation daily for over fifty years. *Meditation for Starters* is available as a book & CD set, book & cassette set, and as a video. Each item is also sold separately.

Yoga for Starters
Gyandev McCord

A unique and innovative introduction to this popular topic, *Yoga for Starters* is a handy lay-flat reference book that covers the basic principles of yoga. Includes sections on standing poses, relaxation poses, spinal stretches, inverted and sitting poses, all with photographs. Also includes suggestions for routines of varying lengths from beginning to advanced study. Most importantly, *Yoga for Starters* gives a broad overview of what yoga is and the main principles and practices associated with it. In addition to a section on yoga postures, there are also chapters on yoga philosophy, breathing, healing principles, and meditation.

Intuition for Starters
J. Donald Walters

Every day we are confronted with difficult problems and thorny situations for which we either don't have enough information to make clear-cut decisions or for which there is no easy intellectual answer. At these moments, we all wish that there was another way to know how to make the right choice. Fortunately, there is another way: through using our intuition. More than just a "feeling" or a guess, true intuition is one of the most important—yet often least developed—of our human faculties. Often thought of as something vague and undefinable, many people mistakenly assume that intuition cannot be understood and developed. *Intuition for Starters* will explain what true intuition is, where it comes from, the practices and attitudes necessary for developing it, and how to tap into intuitive guidance at will.

Chakras for Starters
Savitri Simpson

Long a popular subject in metaphysical and Eastern spirituality circles, interest in the chakras has recently spread into the mainstream. Yet, for all of the newfound interest, until now, there has yet to be written a concise, easy-to-read guide to this most intriguing of all topics. In *Chakras for Starters*, Savitri Simpson demystifies and explains what chakras are, how to work with them, and the benefits accrued from doing so. Readers will learn how working with the chakras can help them feel a greater sense of security, self-control, heartfulness, centeredness, intuition, and spiritual transformation.

Vegetarian Cooking for Starters
Blanche Agassy McCord

Interest in vegetarian eating has been exploding across the country over the last decade. Even many of those who may not want to eat a completely vegetarian diet now recognize that healthy living requires the incorporation of at least some vegetarian principles and foods into their diets. Yet, many of us are still confused by the different theories, fads, and techniques championed by various proponents of healthy eating. In *Vegetarian Cooking for Starters*, Blanche McCord gives straightforward, easy-to-follow dietary advice, immediately useful explanations on how to prepare basic ingredients for cooking, and simple but delicious recipes that will quickly help you incorporate vegetarian meals into your diet.

Resources

❖

Additional Selections from Crystal Clarity

Awaken to Superconsciousness
Meditation for Inner Peace, Intuitive Guidance,
and Greater Awareness
J. Donald Walters

Many people have experienced moments of raised consciousness and enlightenment—or superconsciousness—but do not know how to purposely enter such an exalted state. Superconsciousness is the hidden mechanism at work behind intuition, spiritual and physical healing, successful problem solving, and finding deep, lasting joy. Walters shares his knowledge of the ancient yoga tradition, explains how to apply yoga principles to daily life, describes how to attain inner peace, and provides inspiring meditative exercises.

Money Magnetism
How to Attract What You Need When You Need It
J. Donald Walters

Offering simple but powerful techniques for attracting material and spiritual success, *Money Magnetism* is a practical, easy-to-understand guide, sure to produce results. Filled with fresh, new insights about how to attract true wealth, *Money Magnetism* goes far beyond the scope of other books: each of the principles can not only be used for wealth building but will also help you attract whatever you need in life, whenever you need it.

Affirmations for Self-Healing
J. Donald Walters

This inspirational book contains 52 affirmations and prayers, each devoted to improving a quality in ourselves. Strengthen your will power, cultivate forgiveness, patience, health, and enthusiasm. A powerful tool for transformation.

MUSIC FROM CLARITY SOUND & LIGHT

Music to Awaken Superconsciousness
Experience Inner Peace, Intuitive Guidance,
and Higher Awareness
Donald Walters

Each of the lush instrumental selections on this recording is designed to help listeners more easily access higher states of awareness: deep calmness, intuition, joy, radiant health, and transcendence. Instruction in the liner notes guides listeners on how to actively achieve supercsonsciousness; or, it can be used simply as background music for relaxation and meditation.

Relax
Meditations for Piano
David Miller

Let peace gently enfold you as you listen to these lilting melodies. This soothing instrumental music is the perfect antidote to stress of all types. Calming and inspiring, it will lift you above day-to-day worries and cares. Play it after work, before falling asleep or anytime you want to banish tensions and troubles.

Secrets of Love
Melodies to Open Your Heart
Donald Walters

Unlike any music you have ever heard, *Secrets of Love* will transform your life. Each musical selection captures the essence of one of the many aspects of love. Perfect as background music, "mood" music, or music for relaxation, all eighteen songs can also be actively used as dynamic tools for awakening the loving qualities within your heart.

Mystic Harp 2
Derek Bell

Derek Bell is the legendary harpist of The Chieftains. Original melodies by Donald Walters capture the mystical quality of traditional Celtic music. Derek plays Celtic harp on each of the twenty richly orchestrated melodies. A beautiful sequel to the first Bell/Walters best-selling collaboration, *The Mystic Harp*.